ADHD Parenting Guide

How to Promote Better Behavior and Enhance Your Child's Academic and Social Skills

Jordan Waldrop

Copyright © 2019 Jordan Waldrop

All rights reserved.

© COPYRIGHT 2019 BY **JORDAN WALDROP** - ALL RIGHTS RESERVED.

The content contained within this book may not be reproduced, duplicated or transmitted without direct written permission from the author or the publisher.

Under no circumstances will any blame or legal responsibility be held against the publisher, or author, for any damages, reparation, or monetary loss due to the information contained within this book. Either directly or indirectly.

Legal Notice:
This book is copyright protected. This book is only for personal use. You cannot amend, distribute, sell, use, quote or paraphrase any part, or the content within this book, without the consent of the author or publisher.

Disclaimer Notice:
Please note the information contained within this document is for educational and entertainment purposes only. All effort has been executed to present accurate, up to date, and reliable, complete information. No warranties of any kind are declared or implied. Readers acknowledge that the author is not engaging in the rendering of legal, financial, medical or professional advice. The content within this book has been derived from various sources. Please consult a licensed professional before attempting any techniques outlined in this book.

By reading this book, the reader agrees that under no circumstances is the author responsible for any losses, direct or indirect, which are incurred as a result of the use of information contained within this document, including, but not limited to, — errors, omissions, or inaccuracies..

CONTENTS

Introduction	1
1. ADHD in Children and Why to Modify Your Parenting	3
2. Behavior Management --- Rewarding Good Behavior and Addressing Bad Behavior	9
3. Creating a Routine That Is Structured and Manageable	15
4. Managing Aggression and Defiance in Children with ADHD	20
5. Encouraging Exercise	26
6. Encouraging Thinking Out Loud but Also Promoting Waiting Their Turn	32
7. Believing in Your Child and Yourself	36
Conclusion	41
References	43

JORDAN WALDROP

INTRODUCTION

I, too, am a parent of a child with ADHD. The diagnosis that my son had attention deficit hyperactivity disorder, or ADHD, was both a relief and a terrifying prospect. I knew that he was full of excess energy, always climbing up and jumping off of things when he was not supposed to. Oftentimes he would wiggle free from my grasp in the store and bolt for the toy aisle. When I'd catch him and explain that he had to put the toy back on the shelf because we were not buying toys that day, he would have a complete and utter meltdown. I thought that it was just the antics of a rambunctious, sometimes mischievous, young boy. However, when he started school, I quickly realized that he was not functioning in the classroom as well as he should be. His grades were averaging at Ds and Fs; we started to celebrate when he earned Cs. This was disappointing because he truly was a bright kid, but his intelligence was not showing in the classroom. The worst grade of all was his conduct grade. Every day he would come home with a write-up from his teacher, detailing his lack of attention in class, his constant fidgeting, and random bursts of energy. I told myself that this, too, was just a phase that he would grow out of. Often I would see him get so frustrated that he would explode in anger, hitting or punching his siblings or me. His outbursts seemed incongruous to the situations he was reacting to, but still, I believed he would grow out of it.

The next time we visited his pediatrician, I asked him about these symptoms. After a few more visits, we had our diagnosis of ADHD. The pediatrician explained the diagnosis as best he could, but I was so in shock that almost everything went in one ear and out the other. It was so much to absorb; it was so much information that it felt overwhelming. One thing that I did know was that our way of life was about to shift. I soon understood that my son had a different set of specific needs that required specific strategies to help combat his ADHD symptoms, such as inattention, impulsivity, and overactivity. Even though his pediatrician recommended medication, I wanted to explore all my options in regard to treatment.

I spent months researching strategies for treating and managing my son's ADHD symptoms. I talked with his teachers, school nurses, therapists, and friends who had children with ADHD. I read books, web articles, and scholarly journals about the disorder. After many conversations, many months of trial and error, and much additional research, I compiled a list of strategies that worked for my son and our family. It was incredibly exhausting to tinker with different regiments until I found the one that worked best for him. By implementing specific and consistent routines into his everyday life, I slowly began to see signs of improvement in his behavior. Slowly, his grades began to pick up, and his tantrums became less frequent. It is important to recognize that by no means was he cured of his ADHD symptoms — he and I just knew how to better manage them. Equally, there is no one-size-fits-all strategy to manage all of your child's symptoms.

Because each child is different and no one treatment will be effective for every child with ADHD, I have assembled a list of strategies for you to try with your own child. Within this book is a conversation not only about ADHD and possible treatments but also about how the dynamics of your family adjust with this diagnosis and how your life is impacted in ways you may not have thought of. Unfortunately, ADHD affects not only your child but also your entire family. It is important to engage in this conversation with your family so that together you work to manage your child's ADHD and equip your child for a successful future.

1 ADHD IN CHILDREN AND WHY TO MODIFY YOUR PARENTING

You may have recently found yourself trying to navigate your child's newly diagnosed condition of attention deficit hyperactive disorder (ADHD). Perhaps you have heard of this disorder before. Maybe you've had a friend whose child has also been diagnosed. Perhaps this diagnosis was a completely new idea to you. Regardless of whatever background knowledge you have had so far, ADHD is now a part of your child's life and yours, and you may feel overwhelmed by where to go from here. What is important to know is that many families struggle with the diagnosis of ADHD, but by understanding what this disorder is and how it affects your child, you will begin to understand how to best manage your child's symptoms and encourage them to succeed.

Your family physician may have already given you some information about your child's diagnosis of ADHD. To review, ADHD is a condition "characterized by inattention, overactivity, and impulsivity most frequently identified and treated in primary school" (Charach et al., 2011). You may have noticed some of these characteristics in your child before their official diagnosis. They are frequently distracted, unable to complete one task before moving on to the next one, exhibit frequent and unexpected bursts of energy, act without considering the consequences, and are probably quite impatient. Perhaps your child interrupts others when they are speaking to share their own thoughts that are repeatedly unrelated to the conversation. These are all hallmark symptoms of ADHD and behaviors that you must now learn to moderate in your child.

While those aforementioned symptoms are the most well-known, there are many other symptoms of ADHD that your child may exhibit. For instance, children with ADHD may have concurrent oppositional and noncompliant behaviors, such as dramatic emotional outbursts and acts of physical aggression toward you, their siblings, their peers, and other figures of authority (Charach et al., 2011). You are probably familiar with these behaviors already. You're most likely familiar with how embarrassing it is whenever your child has an utter meltdown, complete with kicking and shouts of indignation, in the middle of a store because you told them to be still or wait their turn. Furthermore, it can be painful when your child acts out physically and harms you or a sibling by pinching, biting, hair-pulling, or even slapping, punching, and kicking. These kinds of behaviors may be common in toddlers, but such behaviors become less common and less frequent as the child ages. In the case of children with ADHD, emotional and aggressive outbursts can persist throughout puberty. Because of this, children with ADHD have specific needs that parents must understand and learn to manage. In the upcoming chapters, you will discover the cognitive processes behind your child's defiance, emotional sensitivity, and aggression, and you will learn techniques to manage these symptoms of ADHD.

Another possible challenge for children with ADHD is the symptoms of anxiety that may coincide. Children with ADHD have problems with executive functions, such as working memory, organizational skills, and inhibitory control. When your child has trouble with executive functions, it can be difficult to follow simple routines or complete simple tasks (Hurley, n.d.). Imagine if you could not remember a conversation from 10 minutes ago, could not find the keys you had just put down, or even could not stop yourself from talking while your boss was speaking. These would all be extremely stressful situations for you. It is important to remember that this may be how your child feels, and from those feelings of powerlessness stems anxiety. Furthermore, if your child is consistently reprimanded for these behaviors, they are likely to experience higher levels of stress.

Another reason why this may occur is that children with ADHD also have difficulty regulating their emotions. Psycom's Katie Hurley explains that "ADHD often causes kids to become flooded with emotions, positive or negative, which can be difficult to manage at the moment. If a child is flooded with feelings of anxiety, for example, that child might struggle to make sense of his thoughts and become caught in a cycle of negative and anxious thinking" (n.d.). You can only imagine that unbreakable loop of negative emotions. It can be so scary for a child to experience anxiety and not know how to cope with or vocalize their feelings. Without understanding or help, their anxiety can just keep growing and growing until they erupt in either an emotional or physically aggressive outburst, as was mentioned before. It is important to keep an eye out for any symptoms of anxiety that your child may display. Let's take a look at some common ways in which anxiety manifests itself in children.

Anxiety can manifest itself in many different ways that may seem surprising. Because of this, it is sometimes hard to recognize anxiety in children with ADHD. Some common symptoms of anxiety in children are trouble falling asleep or staying asleep, increased irritability, withdrawing from peers, combativeness, refusing to go or participate in school, acting out or fooling around at school, twirling hair, and picking at skin. It is important to note that these are just a few of the common exhibitions of anxiety in children with ADHD. You know your child best, and any behavior that deviates from their usual behavior should be taken into consideration as possible symptoms of anxiety.

Thinking back, some of your own first memories might have taken place at school, learning to color inside the lines or listening during story time. You most likely had many good memories of elementary school because you did not have to struggle through bouts of inattention, hyperactivity, and impulsivity — the key symptoms of ADHD. Unfortunately, ADHD can transform school from an environment that should be fun into one that is stressful or ripe with sensory overload. Your child's experience with school will be markedly different from yours because of the challenges that this disorder poses. In addition to the learning curve a child endures when entering primary school, a child with ADHD must also learn to cope with their disorder. As you can imagine, this learning process is and will be very difficult for your child and may result in unsatisfactory grades. According to the U.S. Department of Education, students with ADHD may experience "difficulty sustaining attention to a task [that] may contribute to missing important details in assignments, daydreaming during lectures and other activities, and difficulty organizing assignments. Hyperactivity may be expressed in either verbal or physical disruptions in class. Impulsivity may lead to careless errors, responding to questions without fully formulating the best answers, and only attending to activities that are entertaining or novel" (2009).

These are just a few of the common ways ADHD may affect your child when in school. These small schoolwork errors can build up academically and emotionally. Consistently performing poorly on classroom activities or assignments can negatively impact your child's overall grades and negatively affect your child's sense of self and self-esteem. What happens in your child's early educational settings may alter your child's long-term goals and impede their academic success.

Additionally, U.S. Department of Education reports that students with ADHD, as compared to students without ADHD, had "persistent academic difficulties that resulted in the following: lower average marks, more failed grades, more expulsions, increased dropout rates, and a lower rate of college undergraduate completion" (Weiss & Hechtman as cited in Johnston, 2002; Ingersoll, 1988). This can be very difficult for a parent to hear, especially because you want the best for your child. You want your children to succeed in whatever they put their minds to. You want them to feel confident in themselves and about their schoolwork. You want your child to achieve their full potential. It is important to remember that these wishes for your child are not in vain. ADHD makes these goals more difficult to achieve, but it is not impossible. You will have to put in more time and effort into helping your child with ADHD succeed.

In many ways, your child's functionality in their school setting can disrupt their relationship with your family and their peers. Even though this may be a difficult time for you and your child, it is important to remember that your child is being challenged even further because they are struggling not only with their disorder and concurrent learning disabilities but also with their identity and self-image.

Your child will not be able to help but compare themselves to their peers. They will observe how other students can answer questions easily and frequently in class while they cannot. They will observe other children rewarded for good behavior and class participation while they struggle to sit still in their seat and remain quiet while the teacher is speaking. They will see how school comes naturally to their classmates and not to them, but they won't fully understand why. Young children cannot comprehend the cognitive differences between a student without learning disabilities and one with disabilities like those of ADHD. Moreover, they may not be able to identify within themselves that they are struggling more than their peers. They may begin to think that school is too hard for them or that they are dumb and will never succeed. This kind of thinking can be detrimental to their relationship with themselves, with their peers or even siblings, and with their school overall. It is important to have this discussion with your child to ensure that they are aware of their disorder while also introducing strategies to help them overcome their challenges.

As you already know, it will take more effort on your part to promote academic success in your child. You may be wondering how you would even begin doing so. In many ways, your child's functionality in their school setting can disrupt your family and your child's peer relationships. It can be incredibly frustrating to sit at the table to try to get your child to complete their homework after they've just had a full day of having to manage their ADHD symptoms in a classroom setting that does not allow for hyperactivity and inattention.

It can quickly become a tearful shouting match between you and your child as you try to help them solve their math problems, and they completely zoned out through the entire lesson. The math question begins to feel more like a question in a different language, unintelligible to your child, who has missed out on what the learning fundamentals from earlier that day.

Homework and studying can seem like an impossible task where you are responsible for reteaching a lesson that night after a long day for yourself. The prospect of homework can feel even more disparaging when you envision that this could be the routine for the rest of their academic careers. This can put an enormous burden on your shoulders that may lead you to feel anxiety about your child's schoolwork and homework. This feeling of anxiety about your child could negatively affect you and your child's relationship at times. It is understandable to feel this way; you are not the only parent that struggles with these feelings. What is important to remember whenever your relationship to your child is strained is that you will both make it through this. You will find a way to manage and then a way to thrive. You will find that effective collaboration and communication between the home setting and the school setting will provide a much-needed structure in your child's life. Promoting consistency in language, rewards, and reinforcement strategies will make a drastic improvement in your child's sense of self and academic success (U.S. Department of Education, 2009). It takes time, patience, and precise strategies to encourage academic success in your child. In the coming chapters, you will explore some of the techniques you can implement into you and your child's routines.

This is new territory for you, and you may feel overcome by this learning curve. Before we continue, it is important to remember that things will get better. You will learn more about ADHD, more about your child, more about your parenting strengths, and more about how awesome of a parent you are. The worries and self-doubt that seems as immovable as a mountain now will soon become a mere sandcastle at high tide, easily washed away at sea.

The foundations of understanding and the parenting techniques that will be explored in the coming chapters will quickly become second nature to you. By understanding how ADHD affects your child socially, emotionally, and physically, you can tailor your support to their needs and modify your parenting techniques to best suit your child. You will learn how to encourage your child to overcome the symptoms of ADHD in order to fully engage with others and become their best selves. Raising a child with ADHD is hard work, and you may not always feel like you are succeeding at it. Just remember it will only get better (and easier) from here.

2 BEHAVIOR MANAGEMENT — REWARDING GOOD BEHAVIOR AND ADDRESSING BAD BEHAVIOR

Think back to when you were younger. Your parents may have set strict rules for you, such as you cannot leave the table until you ate everything on your plate, even the peas. Perhaps you had to make your bed every morning before getting on the bus for school. Regardless, rules and expectations are a critical part of a child's life. Rules help children understand the world around them, what is acceptable and unacceptable, in order to develop into a functioning member of society. There are expectations for nearly every aspect of your life. You must pay to buy groceries. You must stop at a stop sign if you wish to drive. You must arrive on time for your job. Whether we like it or not, expectations are unavoidable and a major aspect of society. Similarly, there are expectations that you have for your child. Maybe they are some of the same expectations that your parents had for you. Maybe there are more expectations for your own children, maybe less. The bottom line is that there are rules for your child to follow, but normal rulemaking can be near impossible with children with ADHD, depending on the severity of their symptoms.

You may have already experienced this in some capacity. How many times have you told your child with ADHD to clean up their room, and then five minutes later, they are playing with their toys instead? Or perhaps you have explained time and time again that there are no sweets after dinner, yet your child grabs the cookies anyway. Your favorite is most likely when you think your child has enough sense not to run and jump off of the table or something else outrageous but still does it and hurts themselves.

As any parent would, you more than likely address your child's behavior whenever they do not meet your expectations. In a sterner tone, you repeat, "Clean your room," "No sweets after dinner," or even, "Get down from there!" These addresses may send your child into a temper tantrum, which may surprise you or elicit a similarly emotional reaction that may result in the problem remaining unsolved. Their room is still a mess, the cookie has been eaten, and there's a huge knot on your child's forehead. This can be incredibly frustrating as a parent. You may feel overwhelmed and tempted to give up. However, do not give up. Remember that many other parents are going through similar trials with their child and ADHD. Again, you must remember that it only gets better from here.

Also, remember that, because children with ADHD have functionally different brains, you will need to take a different approach to household rulemaking. Dr. Jeanne Segal and Melinda Smith argue that children with ADHD "often don't 'hear' parental instructions, so they don't obey them. They're disorganized and easily distracted, keeping other family members waiting. Or they start projects and forget to finish them — let alone clean up after them. Children with impulsivity issues often interrupt conversations, demand attention at inappropriate times, and speak before they think, saying tactless or embarrassing things. It's often difficult to get them to bed and to sleep. Hyperactive children may tear around the house or even put themselves in physical danger" (2019).

Most of the time, your child is not trying to be deliberately disobedient. They truly do not register the verbal rules you set, or they are so easily diverted from their task that they get absorbed into the next interesting thing in their vicinity. (To be fair, toys are way more fun than cleaning one's room.) Their bouts of hyperactivity and impulsivity do not allow for proper examination of consequences before they leap from the top of your dining-room table. Their brains do not function in the same manner that your brain does or even the brains of your other children who do not struggle with ADHD. It is important to know this before trying to improve your parenting strategies. Even though your child's disorder does make it more difficult to follow instructions or meet expectations, it does not exempt them from these rules.

However, you may find that the way you think about rules must change. In order for you to meet the challenges of raising a child with ADHD, you must be able to master a combination of consistency and compassion (Smith & Segal, 2019). To be consistent is to set clear rules and consequences for your child to obey and steadfastly employ the consequences when necessary. To be compassionate is to guide your child with love, positivity, and understanding. As you read, this may sound very simple. However, you may find that there are many layers of foundation to lay before your child can regularly follow your instructions.

The first step is to explain clearly what is acceptable and what is unacceptable in your household and at school. You may have verbally explained this to your child before, but it does not seem to stick. This is because of ADHD's effect on a child's executive functions, one of them being memory. One strategy to keep your child aware of their behavioral expectations is to make a chart, list, or (if your child does not yet read) a set of pictures that explain in minimal terms what they can and cannot do. Consider posting these visuals around the house, such as in your child's room and other commonly shared spaces. You could also put a copy inside your child's folder for them to reference while at school. By using a visual that can be easily and repeatedly referenced, your child will begin to remember and learn the rules.

Another simple rulemaking strategy is discussing your expectations of your child before the opportunity to disobey is presented. For example, if you are going to the store with your child, discuss with them that their job is to stay with you at all times, use their inside voices, and not ask you to buy them anything outside of what is on the shopping list. If you can discuss with your child that their environment will change but the rules will not, then they can again make the choice to obey or disobey. By repeatedly referencing the list of expectations, your child will begin to take responsibility for their actions because they are confident in their expectations. Once they know the rules, they can choose whether or not to follow them.

The second step is to encourage them. A successful strategy for children with ADHD is encouraging them to follow the rules by rewarding good behavior while also confidently addressing bad behavior in a constructive way. However, with a reward system, it is important to be explicit that they are being rewarded for their specific actions in the store. By clearly connecting their reward with their obedience, your child may begin to consider their rewards before letting their impulsivity make a decision for them. You know your child best and can decide for yourself how to reward good behavior. However, some common reward techniques are rewarding your child with privileges, praise, or activities rather than with food or toys. This can help bolster their self-image instead of creating an unhealthy relationship with food or objects. Also, change rewards frequently so that your ADHD child does not get bored with the same reward over and over. They may lose the motivation to follow your instructions. If visuals and charts seem to remind your child of their successes, make a chart with points or stars awarded for good behavior. Lastly, it is so important to reward work or behavior immediately instead of promising a reward in the future. However, small rewards that scaffold to bigger rewards can also work. Just remember to always follow through with your reward.

Conversely, whenever your child chooses not to obey your rules, you must carry out their consequences with consistency and ensure that the punishment is appropriate to the action. Consequences should be explicit and spelled out in advance. If your child is learning the rules and their correlating punishments, your child's choices to misbehave will carry more weight with them because they knew the rules and the consequences for not following them. Furthermore, these consequences should immediately follow the behavior. This way, the consequences or punishments will emphasize that they are the result of your child's choice to disobey the rule. Some techniques that you can explore to use to discipline your child are time-outs and the removal of privileges as consequences for misbehavior. Perhaps removing your child from the situations and environments that trigger inappropriate behavior could prove helpful.

Another technique is whenever your child misbehaves, ask them what they have done instead. Have your child verbalize their misbehavior and take ownership of their actions. Similarly, to rewarding your child for their good behavior, you must always follow through with a consequence for bad behavior.

Moreover, the consequence should not be purely reactionary on your part but consistent and appropriate to the wrongdoing. Parents of children with ADHD must also modify their own behavior before hoping to modify their child's. Your child's inability to "listen" can be extremely frustrating to you. That frustration can quickly turn to anger, and you may lash out verbally or physically at your child in a measure to teach them that they disobeyed. However, this method is never effective. Parents have more success with changing their child's behavior by setting clear expectations and consequences that are consistently referenced and discussed between parent and child.

Your child's behavior can make you anxious and stressed, but it is important to remember that your child is likely anxious and stressed as well. If you have an emotional explosion as a reaction to their bad behavior, then your child's anxiety is only increased, and that becomes the focus of the situation, not learning that their behavior was unacceptable.

Compassion is the second key element to effectively parenting a child with ADHD. While you must uphold the rules and consequences you set, it is also important to allow for some flexibility. Being too strict or overly rigid may discourage your child. Instead, learn to allow your child to make mistakes because they are still learning how to behave, just as you are still learning to teach them how to behave. By talking about their mistakes after their discipline has been concluded, then both of you can identify where your child went wrong and collaborate on how to act in the future.

The third step to modifying the behavior of your child with ADHD is to promote positivity. When your child is learning about what behaviors are acceptable and unacceptable, it is equally important to remain aware of your child's emotional well-being. As a parent, you are a model for your child's emotional welfare. You can positively influence the symptoms of your child's disorder (Smith & Segal, 2019). By maintaining a positive attitude, you can better meet the challenges of ADHD. When you are calm and focused, you can emotionally connect with your child. This way, you can help them to be calm and focused like you.

It is also important to keep things in perspective. Both you and your child are still learning how to navigate parenting, obedience, and ADHD. Most of your child's behavior is tied to this disorder and their problems with executive functions. Most of the time, your child's behavior is unintentional. Hold on to the fact that your child adores you and you adore them. You may also want to cling to your sense of humor. Your child's unexpected flurry of karate chops in the bread aisle at the store may be embarrassing at that moment but will be a hilarious family story to tell years from now.

Along these same lines, remember not to sweat the small stuff. Be willing to make some compromises with your child. Your child not picking up their laundry is not as big a deal when they have already swept the floors, washed dishes, and completed their homework. It is important not to be a perfectionist when you are parenting a child with ADHD because if you are constantly dissatisfied, you create impossible expectations for your child that could leave them feeling discouraged and unmotivated to follow any instructions. Giving your child some leeway with their expectations may prove beneficial for you and your child.

Lastly, it is so critical to believe in your child. They most likely already struggle with their self-image and self-confidence in the face of their disorder, so it is vital that they feel they have you in their corner to cheer them on. One technique to remind your child that you believe in them is to make a verbal or written list of everything that is positive, unique, and cherished about your child. Celebrate their odd or quirky behaviors and tell them what makes them so awesome. Reiterate that you trust in your child to learn, change, mature, and succeed. Reaffirm this belief in them on a daily basis. Remind them of their importance as you make their lunch or as they begin their homework. By boosting their self-confidence, you can promote behavioral changes within your child.

A cornerstone to meeting the challenges of ADHD is operating with consistency and compassion. By remaining consistent in your expectations of your child's behavior, they begin to learn what the rules are within their environment. They also begin to learn that it is their responsibility to choose to obey the rules or break them. By remaining consistent in addressing good and bad behaviors, your child will understand why it is in their best interest to obey the rules. However, this learning process requires compassion on your part. You should keep in mind your child's emotional well-being not only when disciplining them but also on a regular basis that is not hinged upon their behavior. Remind your child that they are loved and that they are valued.

3 CREATING A ROUTINE THAT IS STRUCTURED AND MANAGEABLE

As you have already learned, creating a routine that is predictable can help your child with inattention and impulsivity. With a detailed and consistent routine, your child can know what is expected of them, how they should behave, and what tasks to complete. However, making a routine for your child can be challenging when they are also struggling with ADHD. Most of the time, ADHD makes small and seemingly easy tasks feel complicated and impossible. When a task is mandatory but your child feels they cannot accomplish it, they may feel defeated and react emotionally. They may experience tasks like these at both school and home. Multiplication problems may seem to them more impossible than flying. Surprisingly, getting ready for bed may feel just as unmanageable for them. For kids with ADHD, complex, multi-stepped tasks must be broken down into smaller, easier-to-accomplish tasks. Furthermore, breaking down these steps will prove to be more effective when your child has the opportunity to collaborate with you in helping to form their own routines and routine breakdowns.

The most difficult time of the day for you may be getting your child ready for the school day. Not only are they reluctant to get out of bed, but they also have no motivation to go to school. I'm sure you can relate. Regardless, you have to wrestle your child out of bed and get them washed, clothed, and fed before they make their way to school. There are days when scraping your nails on a chalkboard would be preferable to getting your child ready for school. What's worse, though, is getting your child ready for bed. It is still a mystery to all parents why this is so, but whatever the reason, your child is most hyperactive whenever they hear the phrase "It's time for bed." Routines can be extremely difficult for parents because your child's ADHD can make simple directions feel like a list that is a mile long. Their inattention, hyperactivity, impulsivity, and troubles with memory can transform a 30-minute task into a two-hour endeavor. For your child's sake and your sanity, it is time to rethink your child's daily rituals and tasks.

The main aspects of your child's day are getting ready for school, doing their homework, eating dinner, and getting ready for bed. These tasks are huge undertakings for kids with ADHD. It is your job to think about the ways you can incentivize these routines to encourage your child to complete them in a timely manner. Take a look at some techniques for implementing an effective routine for your child.

Earlier, you learned how writing down and displaying your expectations for your child could be an effective way to get them to resist their impulsivity and learn good behaviors. Use charts, posters, sticky notes, or other mediums as a way to remind your child of the components of their routine. Use their favorite colors, stickers, or other fun visuals to keep your child engaged. Incentivize completing their tasks by allowing them to "check off" the task by adding a sticker, drawing a checkmark, or crossing off that item from the list. Design whatever visual component that works for you and your child, but remember to make it fun.

For children who struggle with inattention, impulsivity, or organization, it is important to break down each daily ritual into smaller, less complex tasks. When you break down each ritual, be sure to be very explicit in your instructions. You must be very detailed and consistent in your directions. For instance, instead of the instruction to "clean your room," break down the instructions into separate tasks like "Put all your dirty clothes into the laundry basket in the bathroom." Instead of your child overwhelmed with where to start with cleaning their room, they now have a clear and easy-to-achieve task of putting away their dirty clothes. This task is easy to understand and can be done without your help. Whenever children with ADHD can accomplish a task on their own, no matter the size, they feel better about themselves and are more willing to try to complete a consecutive task. It is important to be consistent always by requesting to put their clothes in the bathroom hamper instead of directly into the laundry room.

However, when it comes to a morning routine, you are battling against your child's tiredness and unwillingness to go to school. This is a double whammy that no one likes to greet first thing in the morning, especially before you are properly caffeinated (if that's your thing). During those critical morning hours before school, morale is low and tensions are high, so it is especially important to make these tasks easy to accomplish. Break down your child's morning routine into three separate categories: getting dressed, eating breakfast, and grooming. Break down these tasks even further into three to five subtasks, but remember to make it fun.

For example, in order to complete the "getting dressed" task, your child must wake up; stretch, jump around, or dance for one minute; tell everyone "Good morning"; and then put on their school clothes. Your child's routine has just gotten way more interesting and is now more fun to complete. They can shake off their sleepiness by dancing for a minute and waking up their brains for the day. Furthermore, the task has gotten easier to accomplish because the subtasks are so easy. The very first task of waking up is already completed by the time their eyes are open. You can make these instructions even easier by writing them out and posting them to their bedroom door or bathroom mirror.

Finding the right formula for your child and their routines will take a lot of practice and patience. They will not learn these skills overnight. However, with your positivity and encouragement, your child will more easily form these habits. When they begin to feel like their tasks are easy, they will be more inclined to do them, which will dramatically boost their confidence, and that self-confidence will transfer to their academic tasks as well. However, these routines cannot be made by yourself. To help your child develop this habit of accomplishing their routines, allow them to help you make smaller task breakdowns.

It is so important to give your child ownership of their routines. This responsibility can improve their behavior and ability to focus. It also boosts their self-esteem. Your child struggles with the ability to manage themselves and find it challenging to resist impulsive behaviors that prevent them from focusing and finishing the task at hand. Help them by encouraging them to create a set of instructions that will be easy for them to complete. However, it would be a good idea to give them choices if they cannot generate ideas on their own.

Offering binary choices in collaboration may be more manageable for them. For example, when it comes to homework, tell them they have some options. Would they like to start their homework immediately when they get home to get it out of the way, or would they rather have an hour to unwind and play? Do not be surprised if they choose the latter. Furthermore, would they like to ride their bikes or play tag for their hour of playtime? Would they like to have an afternoon snack before or after doing homework? Would they prefer a sweet snack or a salty snack? Would they like to complete their math or reading homework first, social studies or science?

Once they have these choices before them, it will be easier to help you form their routines. After that, your child will know that when they get home from school, they will take off their backpack and play outside where they will ride their bikes for an hour. Then they will have an apple and some water as their afternoon snack. Finally, they will complete their math, reading, science, and social studies homework in that order.

It may seem controlling to give your child such a regimented routine, but because of your child's ADHD, a detailed ritual can help them remember their own daily expectations and instructions while simultaneously teaching them skills to better the executive function that they will need for the rest of their lives.

If your child resists their routines, find some other ways to incentivize completing their tasks. Though it may not seem like it, praising your child is one of the most effective ways to encourage them. Be detailed and generous in your praise. Instead of a simple "Good job," take the time to say, "I am impressed with how well you picked up your toys today. I'm very proud of you." By being detailed, you are expressing your appreciation and love for your child when you say you are impressed or proud of them. Furthermore, you are clueing them in to which behavior they did well so that they can strive to repeat it and transfer that before over to other tasks in their life. Also, praise their effort. It is not only about completion but also about having the will to try and complete it. The determination to try is sometimes hard to muster when you are battling ADHD. Encourage your child to keep trying by saying something like, "I appreciate you trying to put your toys away. Now, let's try and put them all away." Praise like this emphasizes that any amount of effort is valid and appreciated and will prove to be effective in fostering their drive to complete their tasks.

If praise is not as effective as you would like it to be, explore other options that are immediately gratifying. When your child has finished all of their homework, they can have five extra minutes of free time before dinner. Or perhaps after they have finished their bedtime routine in full, they can read a story before bed.

Another method would be to set long-term goal rewards along with short-term goal rewards. For instance, if your child completes their homework routine for the whole week, they can choose the movie night for that week. Get creative with your incentives and always keep them rotating so that your child does not get bored. Moreover, as I've said earlier, be sure to avoid rewards like food or toys because your child may begin to develop an unhealthy dependency on food and material objects.

By setting a routine for your child that is consistent and regulated, your child learns that structure is beneficial to them and that they can create self-regulatory structures for themselves for the rest of their lives. When you break down complex daily rituals into smaller tasks that are easy to accomplish, your child is no longer intimidated by the instruction and has an easier way to begin completing it.

It would be a good idea to visually list your child's tasks somewhere that they would frequently see them. This way, their expectations are reinforced throughout the day. This gives your child a sense of ownership over their lives, which can lead to boosting their self-confidence, instead of just being told what to do. Remember to make these tasks fun and let them in on the planning process too. By making these tasks personal and fun, your child will be less likely to resist them. This process of implementing structured routines into your child's life and yours will not be easy, nor will it be quick. This process takes time, energy, patience, and positivity.

4 MANAGING AGGRESSION AND DEFIANCE IN CHILDREN WITH ADHD

Because ADHD affects the behavior of your child drastically, you have explored many techniques and strategies for addressing behavior in your child. However, there is a difference between misbehaving and aggression. To return to the previous example, if your child does not listen to you at the store and throws a tantrum in an effort to persuade you to get them a toy, that is misbehaving. However, if upon refusing to buy the toy your child throws a tantrum and then rushes over to slap your arm, it is a sign of aggression, which can be a more serious concurrent issue alongside ADHD.

No one wants to experience their child attack them out of malice, be it physically or verbally. Your child is one of the most important relationships you have, and it's painful when they get so angry that they say or do things to hurt you. Unfortunately, that is the process of aggression. Dr. Birgit H. Amann and Dr. Keith E. Saylor define aggression as "Behavior with the immediate intent to cause harm — whether to self, others, objects, or property" (2016). This type of behavior is very common in children in the nonverbal age range. Once they can use language, the frequency of aggressive behavior typically decreases. However, children with ADHD inherently have trouble monitoring their emotions, and when compounded with their lack of impulse control, it creates a perfect storm of physically aggressive behavior in children with ADHD at any age. Your child can get so frustrated with themselves, with their surroundings, or with you that the only way to communicate is to explode and try to get you to feel their same irritation.

Sometimes your child's outbursts are surprising, and sometimes you can feel when they are about to erupt. As they sit playing their video game, you tell them to turn it off and get ready for bed. There are a few moments that seem to last forever, and then you know that there is an argument about to erupt. When it does, perhaps there is a barrage of hateful words, kicking, screaming, throwing of toys, and slamming of doors. You may have experienced this exact situation or one similar where your child is openly defiant and aggressive toward you or your rules. It can seem so hopeless when each night brings about a similar tantrum. However, in order to manage your child's aggression, you must first understand where it is stemming.

It is important that your child's difficulty focusing and controlling their actions can affect them in ways you may not expect. Caroline Miller of the Child Mind Institute says, "Tantrums and defiance are not symptoms of ADHD itself, but they are often a result of ADHD symptoms. Inattention and impulsivity can make it very difficult for kids to tolerate tasks that are repetitive, or take a lot of work, or kids find boring. Children with ADHD can be overwhelmed with frustration, and throwing a shoe or pushing someone or yelling 'Shut up!' can be the result of impulsivity. They are less able than other kids their age to manage powerful feelings without an outburst" (n.d.).

It is true that noncompliant behaviors are not symptoms of this disorder, but they sometimes exist concurrently, each feeding off the other. Imagine your brain is going a million miles an hour, jumping from one point of interest to another in your environment, only for your teacher or parent to order you to figure out a math problem. However, you were not paying attention to the math lesson, and you have no idea how to solve the math problem. Now, everyone is looking at you, and you feel so angry at yourself for not being able to pay attention, angry at the teacher for calling on you, and angry at your peers for looking at your expectantly when you have nothing to say.

This is an overwhelming situation for a young child, and it's a situation that could end in a tantrum or an emotional or aggressive outburst. In no way is aggressive or defiant behavior acceptable, but it is understandable. Feelings of aggression can stem from feelings of confusion or inferiority that are brought on by ADHD. Furthermore, if a child is being told from a young age that their brain does not work as it should and their resulting behavior is wrong, it is no surprise that the child would internalize these words and begin to think that there really is something wrong with them, and they would react aggressively when someone reinforced this idea

(Miller, n.d.). It is not a mystery where the aggression comes from, but that does not make it acceptable behavior.

If you think that your child may be harboring aggression or exhibiting signs of aggression, then you should know that early intervention is key. Addressing your child's defiance needs to be of the utmost importance to you. Not only will it be easier for you as a parent, but it could also possibly be the difference between raising a successful adult and raising an unsuccessful one. It is not wise to avoid addressing this issue. These behaviors are not something they "grow out of." In fact, allowing aggressive and defiant behavior to persist can damage their sense of self-control and can alter their sense of right and wrong. That moral compass is what they carry with them throughout their life, so it is important to calibrate it early before their frustrations begin to make choices for them. They should not grow up thinking that unregulated emotions are normal and acceptable. Luckily, there are strategies and techniques that you can try to implement into your child's life to manage their aggression, but it may take a few tries (and a lot of patience) before you find a solution that is right for you and your child.

As you have discovered, repetitive or boring tasks require quite a lot of effort from kids with ADHD. They will want to resist these sorts of tasks, especially if it is instead of something more fun, like playing. Alas, most of these boring tasks are schoolwork, homework, or household chores — all necessary tasks to be completed by your child. Getting dressed for school, picking up toys, and getting ready for bed can feel more like getting ready for battle. It would be so much easier to just throw up your white flag and say, "Forget it, go to bed when you feel like it." It would be so easy to wash your hands of the drama and the fighting and wholly avoid the problem.

Unfortunately for you, these tantrums, arguments, and other overt acts of defiance are your child's way to grapple for the power you hold. If you give in and allow your child to consistently disobey the rules you have set, then you are forfeiting your power as their parent. Once children realize this, they will continue their methods of defiance and aggression to get their way with things. You need to equip yourself with some strategies to mediate these situations.

The first thing to remember when trying to manage your child's aggression or outburst is that losing your own temper never works. Perhaps this method is effective with children who rarely misbehave, but kids who frequently misbehave and are often yelled at begin to ignore it. They begin to think that, because they experience so much yelling, that is the normal way to communicate your frustrations.

When yelling becomes normalized, then your child begins to do it more often and stop paying attention to you raising your own voice as a disciplinary measure. Further down the road, your child will only know to communicate their complex feelings through yelling, be it at loved ones or bosses and coworkers. Before you even begin to try to fix the situation at hand, remind yourself how important it is that you remain calm.

Similarly, with children that frequently misbehave, punishment loses its effectiveness. Children begin to feel as if punishments don't matter. Because they are living in a constant state of punishment, it will not really matter to them to be punished some more (Miller, n.d.). If punishment does not work, what will?

It goes back to laying out the rules very clearly. Kids with ADHD need more structure than other kids, specifically clearer instruction with what behavior is allowed and prohibited. Additionally, opportunities for praise and positive reinforcement prove to be highly effective. Having healthy and affirming relationships between parents and their kids is a powerful tool for moderating disruptive and defiant behavior. If mutual trust is present between you and your child, your child will be more reluctant to break your trust by defiantly acting out. However, the building or repairing of this trust may take some time. In the meanwhile, there are some faster-acting techniques to help your child self-regulate their aggression.

When your child is having a tantrum, they are highly upset. They are most likely crying, perhaps accompanied by some physical movements. There are techniques for you to use as the parent as well as techniques for them to use. When you enter the scene of an upset or irate child, you already know that you should keep your composure and try to initiate communication. Some ways to do this would be to get on the same level as the child and to use friendly eye contact and soft gestures to draw the child's attention toward you.

If they are angry, it may be best to just gesture instead of touching them right away. Next, talk to them in a firm but still, kind voice to ask them how you can help them work through their emotions. If you have developed signal phrases with your child that work to calm them, this would be a good time to use them. Otherwise, encourage them by saying that everyone gets angry sometimes, even you, and everyone must have the courage to move through those emotions.

Another method would be to distract them by redirecting their attention to a bird outside the window or their favorite program on the TV. Here you are trying to encourage them to move on to more productive ways of releasing their emotions. Your job is to be a calming presence and to deescalate the situation.

The next step is introducing self-soothing techniques for your child to turn to in times of distress. These are the techniques that may require some trial and error and, most of all, practice. These techniques may not work the first few times you try them, but these techniques are not miracle solutions. They are strategies to teach your child so they can better regulate their emotions in the future. Some self-soothing strategies to try would be to have your child breathe through their nose to a count of four and then exhale through their mouth to a count of eight. This breathing exercise increases oxygen transport to the brain, soothing your child.

Another technique would be to drink water. It seems simple enough, but a child cannot cry or scream when they are drinking, so it forces them to calm down enough to drink the water in front of them. There are also tactile techniques that your child can turn to, such as playing with playdough, tying knots in a string, or playing with warm water. If their attention is redirected to an interesting activity that requires them to focus, then they can begin to calm themselves.

This next technique requires more planning, practice, and patience; however, it has been proven to be a helpful therapy for many kids who struggle with managing their emotions. To help your child calm down, create a safe space for your child to retreat to where they can have comfort objects, such as pillows, blankets, and plush or squishy toys. This needs to be a safe and private space, such as a large box or some kind of enclosure or even a corner. This safe space needs to be a haven for your child to turn to in order to calm themselves.

More advanced techniques would be to desensitize them from their stressful environment by applying pressure to their body — for example, gently pushing down on their shoulders and arms, squeezing their hands and feet, wrapping them in a bear hug, applying an ACE bandage wrap, or covering them in a weighted blanket. However, these strategies are to be used whenever you have established a strong trust with each other during tense situations; these advanced techniques are to be built up to.

Remember that after your child has calmed down, there is still work to be done. Once they have calmed down to the point where they can speak rationally, you and your child must communicate with each other on the situation that just transpired. Have your child talk about what upset them and caused them to lose their temper. Ask them to name the emotions that they felt and why they think their actions are unacceptable. Have your child relay to you what helped them calm down if there is anything you can do together to prevent another meltdown from happening.

It is important to compound the soothing techniques with a discussion about how the situation escalated to this. Hopefully, this will help your child to connect their actions with their lack of impulse control and trouble with emotion regulation to adopt more helpful and constructive ways of communicating their feelings.

However, sometimes these techniques do not work. Sometimes a child's aggression is so severe that other measures need to be taken. If a child's aggression and defiance are worsening, take a look into counseling, therapy, or your child's primary care physician. Sometimes you may need to turn to a professional who can offer more advanced solutions tailored to your child. They may also be able to help you reconcile your child's aggression because your child's defiance does eventually take an emotional toll on you as well. There should not be any sense of failure with turning to therapy as it is a truly helpful method to help you and your child deal with aggression as a result of their ADHD. Furthermore, your doctor may also be able to offer more solutions and point you in the direction of child therapists, counselors, or even certain medications.

It is important to demonstrate empathy every step of the way when raising a child with ADHD. This disorder affects your child with a variety of symptoms that are sometimes invisible or working in ways that are not always clear. It is important to have an open line of communication with your child, especially if they are demonstrating concurrent symptoms of aggression or defiance. Setting clear expectations for behavior can help your child recognize their choices to behave incorrectly, which may help decrease the frequency of tantrums. However, when your child does act aggressively, it is important to practice techniques to help soothe them.

5 ENCOURAGING EXERCISE

Think about the last time you were physically active. Perhaps running is your favorite way to exercise. Maybe cardio is not your thing, but yoga hits the spot. Maybe you have a consistent exercise routine, or you sneak it in when you can. Whatever your physical activity, exercise makes you feel good. Sure, your legs probably hurt, or your lungs sometimes burn. But overall, exercise does a lot to promote emotional and physical health. Physical activity can get your brain motivated for tasks that require focus. It can give you more energy and help promote mental clarity. Exercise can also help manage symptoms of ADHD in your child.

Think about it — one of your child's problems is the hyperactivity aspect of ADHD. Most of the time, you cannot keep them still. They are squirming in desks, running in the house, jumping, racing, skipping, shouting, and everything in between. They have loads of energy that they are instructed to keep bottled up throughout the day. They are constantly wrestling with the pent-up energy, and when they get home, it needs to be released. The simplest advice to offer would be to let them play, as exercise has many hidden benefits for children with ADHD.

Promoting physical activity can lessen many of the symptoms of ADHD by improving focus. It can also reduce impulsivity in your child. Rae Jacobson of Child Mind Institute reports that "for kids between kindergarten and second grade, as little as a half-hour a day of moderate to vigorous exercise had a positive, measurable impact on their focus and mood [and] showed improved cognitive functioning" (n.d.). A half-hour a day is the time it takes to watch an episode of your child's favorite TV show. Instead of sitting in front of the TV, your child can run around outside for the same amount of time and reap way more benefits. By getting their heart rate up and giving in to their hyperactive impulses for half an hour (or more!), your child can improve their brainpower.

The types of exercises that will possibly generate these improvements are cardiovascular and aerobic exercises. These types of activity elevate one's heart rate and breathing rate for extended periods of time, and they are moderately or vigorously intense. Examples of cardiovascular exercises are running, cycling, and swimming. When you get your body active, your brain has a surprising reaction. Exercise is proven to trigger the brain to release endorphins, which are hormones that flood your body with positive feelings. The feeling that follows an intense workout is often described as "euphoric" and is commonly referred to as a "runner's high" (Bhandari, 2018). These endorphins can drastically improve your child's mood, reduce their frustrations and aggression, and minimize their feelings of anxiety. In addition, the Center for Disease Control (CDC) reports that kids who engage in regular cardiovascular exercises have lower rates of obesity, anxiety, and stress. They are also less likely to develop health problems later on in life. In fact, by creating an exercise routine in childhood, you help your child develop good habits that will carry over into adulthood (Jacobsen, n.d.).

In many ways, exercise acts as a drug on your child's brain. It provides a release for their suppressed energy and impulses and offers a rush of positive feelings. One of the endorphins released during vigorous exercise is dopamine. WebMD reports that "people with ADHD often have less dopamine than usual in their brain [and furthermore] medicines that are often used to treat ADHD work by increasing the availability of dopamine in the brain" (2019). Since dopamine is used to treat symptoms of ADHD and exercise produces dopamine naturally, it is not surprising that exercise can be used as a treatment option of ADHD.

Exercise is a do-no-harm type of treatment for ADHD. This means that when you use the proper precautions for physical activity, there are no adverse side effects to it. There are only benefits to physical activity; therefore, this is a low-risk treatment option for children struggling with ADHD. By creating an exercise routine for your child, you are helping them boost their mental and physical health. In fact, creating an exercise routine that the whole family could take part in can benefit everyone in the long run.

Making daily exercise a part of your family's routine can strengthen your bond as a unit and also promote a healthy lifestyle for yourself and your other children. Imagine how good it must feel for your child to see their whole family physically engaging with them, understanding the need for bottled-up energy to be released. Additionally, the surge of dopamine and other endorphins promotes bonding within your family when you all exercise together. This small exercise routine can significantly bolster your child's confidence and self-image and work through any remaining anxiety that they have been harboring from the day. This small act of support can remind your child that their family has their back and are there to help them whenever needed, an act that hopefully reduces the chances of your child's emotional outbursts when they feel frustrated.

Another fantastic reason to exercise as a family is that you are encouraging the overall health of your family. You yourself may deal with a lot of stress just from trying to successfully parent a child with ADHD. Parenting a child with a disability requires specific attention not only toward your child but toward yourself too.

Envision this workout time as an act of self-care where you can focus on de-stressing and working through your own negative emotions. Your partner or other children may be dealing with their own stresses that they have not verbalized. Including your entire family in a workout can encourage everyone to burn through the baggage left over from the day and renew themselves in a post-workout rush of endorphins. You may find that your family dynamics improve when you exercise as a family in the way that you create new memories and strengthen familial bonds.

Whether or not you choose to include the rest of your family, it is important to remember the value of structure and routines in your child's exercise. If you can remember, it is critical to be both consistent and compassionate when you impose a routine. One strategy to help with consistency is setting a time during the day that is accessible and logical for you and your child. If neither you nor your child is a morning person, then exercising before school or work may not be a good fit for you. If you think that your child may benefit from exercising before starting homework, then set that time and stick to it. Every morning or afternoon, your child will begin to depend on that release of energy and quickly adopt it into their routine.

Though you are trying to stay consistent with the workout, it is wise to keep it varied too — for example, Monday's activity could be jogging around the neighborhood, Tuesday's activity could be dancing to their favorite songs for the whole thirty minutes, and Friday's special activity could be going to the park for an hour. By keeping the activities fresh but still maintaining a schedule, your child can reap the cognitive benefits of exercise while also practicing following instructions similar to their other routines.

Occasionally, there will be days when your child does not wish to be active. This is where compassion comes back into the conversation. While sometimes they may not wish to be active, you can consider exercise as a type of therapy or treatment that works best when employed regularly if not daily. However, if your child does not want to exercise one day, empathize with them. Ask them if there is anything on their mind that may have them down or stressed. Talk to them about the importance of exercise so that their body and brain are in tip-top shape. Most of all, show understanding so that they do not feel like they are failing because they do not want to exercise.

More likely than not, though, they may be bored with their routine. When you suspect your child is resisting exercise because they're bored, here are some other ways to get your child active. If you've been doing a lot of walking, jogging, running, and biking, consider taking out those roller blades that have been in the garage forever. Or perhaps find a local pool or swimming hole and swim laps. Take it a step further by introducing simple strength training exercises, like lunges, squats, push-ups, pull-ups, and minimal and appropriate weightlifting. If your child is ready for more complex exercises, consider rock climbing, dance, gymnastics, or yoga.

Furthermore, we live in a world where nearly everything is accessible online. Search YouTube for martial arts training videos to focus on skills like focus and concentration, general balance, memory, consequences of actions, and fine motor skills (WebMD, 2017). Whatever you decide to do to spice up your child's workout, allow it to be a collaborative effort so that they will be more inclined to exercise.

Another way for your child to get active is to engage them in team sports. However, for kids with ADHD, this type of environment may prove difficult, so it is important to understand the limitations of your child before you enroll them in any team sport. Child Mind Institute's Rae Jacobson argues that "for a lot of kids, including some with ADHD or other learning challenges, gym class — if they still have it — is the worst part of the day. Organized sports are minefields of potential embarrassment for kids who struggle to remember multi-step directions, aren't comfortable with physical contact or just aren't as coordinated as their peers. Making exercise appealing to children who'd rather sit in the bleachers is a challenge" (n.d.).

Whenever children with ADHD are put in a situation where they must perform in front of peers and other figures of authority, it can be incredibly anxiety-inducing. Similar to when they are in school, they will be comparing themselves to other children without disabilities and feeling inferior. Children with ADHD may have trouble memorizing football plays and what techniques they worked on at their last soccer practice. They may even lose focus and pick flowers in the outfield and, therefore, bungle the play. This can be both devastating and mortifying for some children struggling with ADHD. It is important to know your child and know whether a competitive team sport would be beneficial to them.

Typically, competitive sports are not the best choice for kids with ADHD because they innately have a hard time following directions or are not as coordinated as their peers. This is okay. There are plenty of non- or less-competitive team sports that your child can try on and decide for themselves if it is a comfortable fit.

Ideally, you want to find a sport that still raises your child's heart rate without stressing them out. As mentioned before, swimming and martial arts are great options for kids who are not equipped or ready for competitive team sports. Some other great options are track, fencing, kayaking or canoeing, archery, hiking, surfing, and skateboarding. All these sports can be practiced in a team setting but do not invite the same type of competition. Instead of peer to peer, your child is actually challenging themselves. These non-competitive sports encourage your child to better themselves in an environment that is not as stressful yet still provides cardiovascular exercise to lessen the symptoms of ADHD.

It is important to encourage your child to find a sport or activity that suits them. Children who find enjoyment in their activities are less likely to get bored and resist exercise, and they are more likely to stay active as they get older. It can be very easy to integrate exercise into your child's daily routine as long as you remain consistent and compassionate. Be diligent and stick to the exercise routine that you outlined but remain sensitive to adjustments you may need to make based on your child's willingness and enjoyment of the activity.

One way to encourage them to stay consistent with their exercise is to include the whole family in the activity. Take family bike rides. Walk to school or to the bus stop. Even just a game of tag in the front yard can get the whole family moving and strengthening their bond.

Exercise is such a useful method for reducing some of the symptoms of ADHD, which included little to no monetary cost. It also poses virtually no risk to your child as some other medications or alternative treatments might. Getting your child physically active can improve their cognitive function and help them work through their disorder without them being conscious that they are engaging in a type of therapy or treatment. While exercise may not work for all families, it is an easy and low-risk option to try.

6 ENCOURAGING THINKING OUT LOUD BUT ALSO PROMOTING WAITING THEIR TURN

You may be wondering why on earth anyone would be recommending that a child with ADHD be encouraged to think out loud. Is that not one of the biggest problems you are facing? It is true that children with ADHD will often say things out of turn or act without permission, which causes rifts in their environments and settings such as school or public spaces. When your child is in one of these settings or even at home, they have a very specific set of instructions that they are supposed to adhere to. Whenever they speak or act out of turn, they are typically not following that instruction and landing themselves in trouble. So far, we are on the same page. However, thinking out loud is a little different. Because your child acts or speaks impulsively, you have seen it frequently land them in trouble. However, by encouraging them to think out loud, you can get a better sense of your child's thought process and can, therefore, help them control their impulsivity. Learning to wait their turn before speaking is an important skill that can be taught alongside thinking out loud.

Once you and your child have worked on moderating their impulsivity, you can begin to teach the skill of learning to wait their turn, which is a very important skill for the rest of their life. As you are most likely well aware, children with ADHD lack self-control. As a result, often they are acting, speaking, jumping, dancing, throwing things, and everything else under the sun before thinking through their possible consequences.

Children with ADHD rarely have the ability to process their thoughts or actions before speaking or acting on them. It is these actions of interrupting or knocking over supplies that most likely earn results in numerous behavioral write-ups in your child's take-home folder and a rapidly declining conduct grade. Learning to think through consequences is an important skill that your child will need to adopt so that they are successful students and eventually competent adults. In order to learn this skill, one technique is to encourage thinking out loud.

When your child is encouraged to think out loud, it means that you are stopping them before they interrupt or misbehave, and you ask them to walk you through their thought process to tell you why they would do what they were about to do. For instance, if they are about to throw a toy at their sibling, you will stop them before this happens and ask them why they thought throwing a toy was an appropriate response to the frustration that they were feeling. You might ask, "What did your sibling do to make you angry?" Your child may not be able to answer this right away, and this is where your help comes in. Try to help them find the words to communicate clearly the emotion that they're feeling. The action of throwing is prompted by a certain emotion. Perhaps that emotion is anger, frustration, sadness, dejection, or even embarrassment. Your child is probably already aware of some of these emotions, but it's your job now to connect the action they were going to take with the emotion that they felt so that they can analyze what they were feeling and learn how to address that emotion better.

The next step is to ask what other ways they can communicate this emotion that would not be an act of violence. Together, you can come up with a list of possible reactions that are healthy and productive, such as telling an adult that someone has hurt their feelings, addressing that person themselves, and telling them what they felt in a calm tone. Perhaps if your child is at an age where they can write sentences, have them write a letter that expresses their feelings and have them deliver it to that person.

The last step is to discuss why an act of violence would not be appropriate for the situation. Talk to them about how their actions can affect the feelings of others. This skill is especially important for their school setting. For example, the next time, it may be a fellow classmate that they are angry at. Hitting a peer could be of a more severe consequence. However, when they are angry at home, it is important for them to associate their thinking-out-loud skills with what they can do in the classroom. Not only is this skill useful for preventing possible violent reactions from your child, but it can also be appropriate for preventing speaking out of turn.

If your child has ADHD, they also have a tough time keeping their comments to themselves while others are speaking. This probably happens a lot in your household. Perhaps you or your partner or one of your children is telling a story at dinner. While they are in the middle of speaking, your child with ADHD may interrupt them with a comment that is not related to the story being told. You were telling a story about a commercial you saw earlier, and your child interrupted you with how they wanted an orange with breakfast tomorrow. Their comment was not related to the story being told at all. This is because your child was enraptured by something else in their environment while you were speaking. They were not focused or even listening to what you were saying. On top of that, they were not asked to speak and actually interrupted the thought of another person.

The next time this happens, take your child aside and go through a similar process with them. Ask if they realize that they were interrupting someone while they were speaking. If they did not realize, tell them to review what just transpired and inform them that they interrupted the thought of another, which is unacceptable behavior. Next, ask them what they were thinking about and to consider whether it related to the story that was being told. Once they realize that their thoughts were not conducive to the conversation being had, ask them what they should have done instead. Discuss with them that in the instance of an unrelated thought popping into their head while someone else is speaking, they should keep it to themselves until it is their turn to share. Discuss with your child that even though their thoughts are valid and others will be interested in hearing what they have to say, it is important to wait their turn to speak. Instruct your child to hold on to their thought, or perhaps write it down if they are easily forgetful and save it until after the speaker is through saying what they had to say. This skill will be especially helpful for school settings when classroom management depends on cooperating with others. For example, when a teacher is giving a lesson, it is very rude to interrupt them. It demonstrates that your child is not engaging with the instruction or lesson.

The final step of the "thinking out loud" learning technique is to encourage your child to be more aware of their surroundings. When they have an unrelated thought, teach them to hold it. Urge them to pause and listen to see if the current conversation would be appropriate for their comment. If not, then they should realize that they have not been paying attention and should start doing so in order not to miss out on anything further.

In the effort to dissuade impulsivity, there are some techniques that you can use to help your child learn to stop interrupting others when they speak. The best method to promote self-control is to practice together the idea of pausing. Similar to the example before, if your child has a thought that they really want to share, have them pause for a second, listen to what is being said, and then determine whether their response is thoughtful or unrelated.

As a parent of a child with ADHD, you want to encourage more thoughtful responses. To practice, ask interactive questions about their homework or perhaps their favorite TV show, video game, or book. When you ask engaging questions, they will be thinking more critically about the subject matter. Ask questions like, "What happened on the last episode of your TV show?" or "What do you think about this character?" or "Why do you think you have to do math homework?"

Strive to ask a few questions with clearly defined answers and some that are open-ended. When you ask them questions about the things they are interested in, they will have an easier time paying attention in your conversation and generating a response that is directly related to what you're asking. This is exactly the skill you want them to learn for the classroom setting. So by asking engaging questions about homework (like their teacher will) or some other point of interest and then asking them to pause and really think about their answer before they give it, you are teaching them the skill of listening to the question being asked, thinking carefully about the subject material, and generating thoughtful replies. These are all skills that are necessary to be active and participatory in classroom settings.

By promoting thoughtfulness before speaking, your child can transfer this skill to the classroom and other aspects of learning, such as waiting and considering all the answers before selecting one on a test. Furthermore, by encouraging your child to be more thoughtful in what they say, you are also teaching them to monitor their self-control. If they can pause long enough and check out how they feel before speaking or acting, then they can begin to increase their emotional intelligence. This means that they can parse out how they feel, assign words to their emotions, and less frequently, resort to violence or emotional outbursts as a means of communication. If they can verbalize their emotions, they can begin to manage their impulsivity, one of the major symptoms of ADHD.

7 BELIEVING IN YOUR CHILD AND YOURSELF

You've learned about the many challenges that come with raising a child with ADHD. In addition to learning disabilities, there are also some emotional problems that your child may encounter, such as anxiety, low self-confidence, and even depression. You never know how this disorder can affect your child, so it is important that you frequently check in with them. Opening up a healthy dialogue with your child about ADHD and the resulting emotional tolls can offer your child support even when you do not realize it. Your child may be experiencing stressors that you may not be aware of. Similarly, you may be experiencing some major stressors in your own life that you need to know how to process.

It is not easy being a parent, and ADHD makes your job even harder. It's difficult to see your child struggle, no matter if you have strategies to help them or not. It's difficult to experience your child get so angry or overwhelmed. As a parent of a child with a disorder or disability, so much of your emotional and mental capacity is given to the needs of your child. However, you have to be able to recognize and address your own needs as well. In order to be the best parent you can be, you must be the best version of yourself. That includes giving yourself the time and space to understand where you are in your personal relationships and your relationship with yourself. You need to carve time out of your day, week, and month for some self-care. When ADHD is a part of your child's life and yours, you must treat yourself and your child with love and care.

As previously discussed, your child may experience an intense array of negative emotions and low self-esteem as a result of their ADHD. Unfortunately, ADHD makes being in a school setting very difficult, and therefore, when your child compares their progress, classroom performance, or grades to that of their peers without learning disabilities, it sometimes generates feelings of inferiority or low self-worth. Your child may not be able to verbalize these feelings to you, and they may suffer through them silently and alone. This skewed sense of self could continue over into their teenage years and adulthood. It is important that you and your child have a conversation about ADHD and how it affects them daily.

It is never too early to begin this type of dialogue. Explain to them what ADHD is, how it makes them different, and how it makes learning different for them. It is important to avoid having your child feel othered or outside of what is normal. Explain to your child that ADHD does not make them "dumb" or "not good at school" but just poses extra challenges that their classmates do not have to face. It is important that they also know that it is possible to manage their symptoms with time and practice, as you've explored throughout these chapters. On the other hand, give your child the space to tell you how ADHD makes them feel and in what ways it affects them. If needed, help them assign words to their feelings; help them name the emotions that are perhaps too complex for them to explain. Opening up a conversation about the symptoms of ADHD can be a helpful tool for you and your child and a way to monitor your child's sense of self.

ADHD changes the ways you parent; it requires more of you and encourages you to explore other avenues with child-rearing. While discussing the various parenting methods and techniques for raising a child with ADHD, it is critical to talk about your mental and emotional needs as well.

As I'm sure you've realized by now, there is no such thing as a perfect parent. You will have your shortcomings. You will say the wrong things and lose your temper (often). You will want to quit at times. Often you will feel like a failure. In those times, it may be comforting to know that all parents feel this way; all parents struggle with inadequacy. No parent is perfect, and sometimes, it just feels good to hear that from someone else.

You are succeeding. No matter how low you feel at times, you are still succeeding. You are succeeding because you love your child, because you are trying to make the best life for them, and because even though you may have struggled or even failed tonight, you are trying again tomorrow.

It does not matter how many times you fail; it's about always trying again. However, it takes a lot of courage and strength to keep getting up every day with the resolve to try again. It can take a toll on you. You need to check in with yourself frequently and give yourself the care and attention you need.

First, find ways to give yourself a break. If you are in the midst of an explosive tantrum with your child, take a moment to step away. Give yourself some time; it can only be a minute or two to compose yourself in the protection of your own private space before going back out there to de-escalate and address the situation at hand.

Breaks should not only be taken when necessary. Schedule some breaks throughout your day. Some can be short; some can be longer. It is important to allow yourself the time you need to decompress from the day and get in touch with your emotional and mental states. The house will not go up in flames if you take some well-deserved personal time.

Second, create a safe space for yourself. Similar to the technique you learned about earlier for your child, it could be useful to create a safe space for yourself in times of need. Your space may be different and comprised of elements outside of stuffed animals, but it's whatever suits you best. Perhaps your safe space contains your favorite blanket or comfiest sweatshirt. Perhaps your comfort objects are your favorite magazine or your journal. Maybe your safe space is your bathroom with candles lit and soft music playing. Your safe space can be anywhere and anything. What is important, though, is that everyone in your family respects your boundaries in regard to this safe space. Make sure your partner and your children appreciate that when you are in your safe space, you are not to be disturbed. You should be able to trust this space as a place designated to peace, privacy, and protection. Set up these boundaries early on, just as you would for your child's safe space.

Third, establish your own positive routine. While your child's routine will intersect with your own for most of the day, you do not have the same routine as them. You must establish your own rituals throughout the day that will promote your own mental health. In the mornings, try devoting thirty minutes or more to yourself before any of your kids wake up. Take this time for yourself. Savor your cup of coffee or tea. Read your favorite book. Journal. Catch up on your favorite TV show. Have breakfast with your partner. Meditate. Work out. Stretch or do yoga. Walk outside and enjoy the sunrise. Take that half-hour and use it to recharge yourself. Show yourself some unadulterated, shameless, and selfish love. You deserve it, and more importantly, you need it. Remember that your identity is more than just a parent. You are a person with emotional needs who deserves them to be fulfilled.

Fourth, understand and respect your limitations. It is key to remember that you cannot do it all. Sometimes you will not operate at your full capacity, and that is more than acceptable. Sometimes you are under the weather, and sometimes you are just simply out of steam, burnt out, and exhausted. Sometimes the dishes will have to wait until tomorrow. Sometimes laundry will pile up. Sometimes you and your kids will go to bed and forget to brush your teeth. All of this is okay. You must learn the limitations of your body and mind in order to maintain your own health and sanity. You must learn when to say no to things like going out with friends or staying late at work. Take the time for yourself without guilt. You owe it to yourself to recuperate whenever you realize you are not feeling like your best self.

Fifth, recognize your successes and congratulate yourself. Similar to how you would respond to your child's successes, celebrate your own victories throughout your day. Focus on the small triumphs, like carving out time to read or remembering to pack your lunch for the day. Identify small wins and honor them as you do with bigger triumphs. Find reasons to reward yourself, like just making it through the week. Show yourself some appreciation by verbally affirming yourself or complimenting yourself. If you feel like it is warranted, buy yourself a little something as a reward. Perhaps there is a pair of earrings you've had your eye on, or you have been eager to try out a new lunch place. Whatever you do, show yourself that you care.

Sixth, assess your relationships. Parenting a child with ADHD can be taxing on not just the relationship with yourself but your relationship with others too. Assess your connections with your partner, friends, and other children. Which relationships need attention? Keep the lines of communication open between you and your partner. Just as ADHD takes a toll on your child and yourself, it takes a toll on your significant other as well.

Check in with them frequently. Ask how they are doing or if you can do anything to help them. It's okay to take the initiative too. Do something thoughtful or make a kind gesture toward your partner to remind them you care about them. Include them in some of your self-care activities and turn them into couples-care activities.

ADHD should not impair your relationship with your partner. On the other hand, if you have other children, be sure to give them the same amount of attention as you do your child with ADHD. Because of ADHD, their livelihoods and routines have also been altered. Talk with them about how these changes may be affecting them. Create special routines for just you and them so that you can build up their relationship with you as well. Furthermore, do not neglect your social spheres. Friends are important to your mental health. It is so important to have ties outside of your family setting. Your friends are a support system that you can turn to when you need, and you for them. However, in order for that system to work, you must not forget to put in the time and effort it takes to keep those friendships strong.

Lastly, find a therapist or community of support. If you ever find that things have become too overwhelming for you to manage on your own, consider seeking professional help. There is no stigma surrounding turning to a counselor or therapist if you feel like you need it. Sometimes you need more assistance than what you or a trusted loved one can provide. Therapy is a valuable asset for parents who feel like they are struggling with the challenges of their child with ADHD. However, if therapy is not for you, try reaching out to a local support group for parents with children with ADHD. You may be able to find more strategies and better techniques from fellow parents than you would with a therapist. Explore some of these options as a way to get even more assistance with learning how to parent your child with ADHD.

While it is important that you remind your child that they are important, loved, and supported, it is also important that you feel this way. It's important that you take care of yourself so that you can take care of your child and their specific needs with ADHD. Once you have properly cared for yourself, you will feel more confident in your parenting skills. In order to teach your child to love themselves, demonstrate that you love and care for your own well-being, and they will follow suit. You are their role model. So by modeling good practices of self-care, you can teach them to assess their well-being too.

CONCLUSION

Parenting a child with ADHD can be tremendously challenging. Children with ADHD often have trouble with simple tasks, such as paying attention in class, controlling what they say and do, organizing their thoughts or tasks, completing simple activities, and regulating their emotions. Oftentimes, they resort to emotional outbursts, overt acts of defiance, and expressions of aggression. They feel like they are not being heard, or perhaps they do not know how to verbalize their feelings. As a child, processing complex emotions can be isolating and overwhelming. Being unable to express themselves can lead to your child experiencing acute anxiety or even depression. These negative feelings can result in poor participation in class, low grades, and feelings of low self-confidence. These negative feelings, in combination with their inattention and impulsivity, can lead to behavioral issues that need to be addressed.

You have explored many strategies to assist you in raising your child with ADHD and addressing their symptoms. You have learned the importance of making your expectations, instructions, and rules very explicit while also clarifying the consequences if those expectations are not met. You have learned how to create manageable routines that can be broken up into smaller, easier-to-complete tasks that encourage your child's focus and attention.

On the other hand, you have discovered the signs of aggression and defiance and explored possible ways to moderate your child's aggression. You have realized how critical exercise is in managing hyperactivity in a child with ADHD and how playtime can be a fun and structured way to reinforce the effectiveness of routines in your child's daily life. You have also learned that to curb your child's impulsivity and improve your child's classroom experience, you may have to help your child talk through their thought processes.

Lastly, you were reminded that you need to care for yourself more. As a parent of a child with ADHD, you endure more stress than most parents without a child with this disorder. You must check in with yourself often and address your own needs so that you can be the best parent you can be.

Remember that it is important to remain consistent in your routines, directions, and discipline while also showing compassion when your child makes mistakes. You and your child are still learning, and you should take care to remember that. Additionally, praise your child often and remind them of how much you love them. Even when it seems very difficult to keep your temper around them, you still need to demonstrate how much you love them. When they feel supported, their self-esteem improves.

At the end of the day, keep in mind that your child did not choose to have ADHD. They are struggling with this disorder more than you are, but together, your bond as parent and child will triumph over ADHD.

You got this. Most of all, remember it all gets better from here.

REFERENCES

Charach, A., Dashti, B., & Carson, P. (2011). Retrieved from https://www.ncbi.nlm.nih.gov/books/NBK82361/

Hurley, K. (2018). Retrieved from https://www.psycom.net/adhd-children-anxiety

Jacobsen, R. (n.d.). Retrieved from https://childmind.org/article/adhd-and-exercise/

Miller, C. (n.d.). Retrieved from https://childmind.org/article/adhd-behavior-problems/

Smith, M., & Segal, J. (2019). Retrieved from https://www.helpguide.org/articles/add-adhd/when-your-child-has-attention-deficit-disorder-adhd.htm

U.S. Department of Education. (2009). Identifying and treating attention deficit hyperactivity disorder: a resource for school and home. Retrieved from https://www2.ed.gov/rschstat/research/pubs/adhd/adhd-identifying_pg4.html

WebMD. (2019). Exercise and depression. Retrieved from https://www.webmd.com/depression/guide/exercise-depression#1

WebMD. (2017). What's the best exercise to manage ADHD? Retrieved from https://www.webmd.com/add-adhd/exercise-manage-adhd-symptoms#1

WebMD. (2018). Adult ADHD and exercise. Retrieved from https://www.webmd.com/add-adhd/adult-adhd-and-exercise#1

www.ingramcontent.com/pod-product-compliance
Lightning Source LLC
Chambersburg PA
CBHW071255070526
44583CB00017B/2479